D1243355

ANIMAL SAFARI

Chimpanzees

by Derek Zobel

BELLWETHER MEDIA • MINNEAPOLIS, MN

Note to Librarians, Teachers, and Parents:

Blastoff! Readers are carefully developed by literacy experts and combine standards-based content with developmentally appropriate text.

Level 1 provides the most support through repetition of high-frequency words, light text, predictable sentence patterns, and strong visual support.

Level 2 offers early readers a bit more challenge through varied simple sentences, increased text load, and less repetition of high-frequency words.

Level 3 advances early-fluent readers toward fluency through increased text and concept load, less reliance on visuals, longer sentences, and more literary language.

Level 4 builds reading stamina by providing more text per page, increased use of punctuation, greater variation in sentence patterns, and increasingly challenging vocabulary.

Level 5 encourages children to move from "learning to read" to "reading to learn" by providing even more text, varied writing styles, and less familiar topics.

Whichever book is right for your reader, Blastoff! Readers are the perfect books to build confidence and encourage a love of reading that will last a lifetime!

This edition first published in 2012 by Bellwether Media, Inc.

No part of this publication may be reproduced in whole or in part without written permission of the publisher. For information regarding permission, write to Bellwether Media, Inc., Attention: Permissions Department, 5357 Penn Avenue South, Minneapolis, MN 55419.

Library of Congress Cataloging-in-Publication Data

Zobel, Derek, 1983-
Chimpanzees / by Derek Zobel.
    p. cm. – (Blastoff! Readers. Animal safari)
Includes bibliographical references and index.
Summary: "Developed by literacy experts for students in kindergarten through grade three, this book introduces chimpanzees to young readers through leveled text and related photos"–Provided by publisher.
ISBN 978-1-60014-602-2 (hardcover : alk. paper)
1. Chimpanzees–Juvenile literature. I. Title.
QL737.P96Z627 2011
599.885–dc22   2011005558

Printed in the United States of America, North Mankato, MN.

080111   1187

Contents

What Are Chimpanzees?

Chimpanzees are **primates**. They are also called chimps.

Chimps have long arms. They walk on their feet and the **knuckles** of their hands.

Where Chimps Live

Chimps live
in grasslands
and forests.
They often build
nests in trees.

Communities

Chimps belong to groups called **communities**.

Most communities have a leader. This chimp is called the **alpha male**.

Every community has a **territory**. Chimps screech and shake branches to keep other animals away.

15

Chimps make
noise to call
to each other.
They grunt and
bang on trees.

Eating

Chimps eat fruits, leaves, and **insects**. They use sticks and rocks to get to food.

This chimp
uses a stick
to find and
eat **termites**.
Smart chimp!

termite nest

Glossary

alpha male—the male chimpanzee that leads a community

communities—groups of chimpanzees

insects—small animals with six legs and hard outer bodies; insect bodies are divided into three parts.

knuckles—rounded areas where bones come together in the hands

primates—animals that use their hands to grasp food and other objects; primates are related to humans.

termites—insects that live in large groups and feed on wood

territory—the area where an animal or group of animals lives and hunts

To Learn More

AT THE LIBRARY

Goodall, Jane. *The Chimpanzee Family Book.* Saxonville, Mass.: Picture Book Studio, 1989.

Kalman, Bobbie, and Hadley Dyer. *Endangered Chimpanzees.* New York, N.Y.: Crabtree Pub. Co., 2005.

Martin, Patricia A. Fink. *Chimpanzees.* New York, N.Y.: Children's Press, 2000.

ON THE WEB

Learning more about chimpanzees is as easy as 1, 2, 3.

1. Go to www.factsurfer.com.

2. Enter "chimpanzees" into the search box.

3. Click the "Surf" button and you will see a list of related Web sites.

With factsurfer.com, finding more information is just a click away.

Index

The images in this book are reproduced through the courtesy of: Eric Isselée, front cover; Tier Und Naturfotografie J & C Sohns / Getty Images, p. 5; Anup Shah / NPL / Minden Pictures, pp. 7, 13; Minden Pictures / Masterfile, pp. 9 (top), 21; Oleg Snameskly, p. 9 (left); Dominique de La Croix, p. 9 (right); Corbis / Photolibrary, p. 11; Suzi Eszterhas / Getty Images, p. 15; Morales Morales / Photolibrary, p. 17; Suzi Eszterhas / Minden Pictures, p. 19 (top); Ricardo Esplana Babor, p. 19 (left); Henry Wilson, p. 19 (middle); Ljupco Smokovski, p. 19 (right).

For Every
Individual...

Renew by Phone
269-5222

Renew on the Web
www.imcpl.org

For General Library Infomation
please call 275-4100